Collection of Poems

With Review

The Argument of Butterflies

"Where the messenger left off"

Brandon Taliaferro

© 2017 Brandon T. Taliaferro

ISBN 10: 0-692-83419-2

ISBN: 13: 978-0-692-83419-0

Published by: Horace P. Publishing

Horace.p.publishing@gmail.com

Printed by: Createspace

<u>Special Thanks</u>

First and foremost I would love to give praise to the Most High for blessing me with the opportunity to share my poetry. According to my mother, I have been writing poems since my youth, by writing Mother's Day cards and such. Poetry has been my outlet, my passions and it has always been my dreams to get them published. I would like to thank my family for all of their support: my father William, my mother Trissy, my brothers Bryan and William III and to all of my family and friends that I have not mentioned. I would like to give thanks to my wife Danielle Taliaferro for her support throughout this process and journey.

This collection of poetry is dedicated to Horace Seaborne.

<u>Table of Contents</u>

<u>The Argument of Butterflies</u>

Where the Messenger Left Off

"By the age of 33 I will leave my message where the messenger left off,

Though I pray he forgives me for my blasphemy."
Brandon Taliaferro

<u>Introduction</u>

What if life had no end and death was just a mere myth? Would we still strive for perfection or just let life pass us by? What if time became less valuable causing everything around it to remain meaningless? The way we work for money would become pointless, having no form to measure labor. The only form we would have is the work itself. Days in and days out would simply rest on the shoulders of the sun, nights would become restless, never feeling the need to race against the rising of the sun and never seeming to grace its setting. Would we say I love you to the ones who mean the most to us, knowing that everyday there is no way they could ever leave us. See, life is the balance of death and death is the existence of life. Ah! Yes I agree with Marcel Proust; we must be threatened by death in order to fully enjoy life. But then that brings up my next question; what exactly is life? Some believe that life is the breath we take each and every single morning, others say that it's the things we accomplish that keeps us living. Some believe it's the cycles we go through from child to man, while others remain clueless…simply living life.

In this book of poems and reviews you will discover my definition of what life deeply entails and what it means to me through my perspectives. In order to do so, we must take a look at a man who has influenced a different way of viewing life. Not only did he cause chaos in the religious communities of his time, but he paved an avenue for scientists to follow. Whether his theories are true or not, his ideals on evolution opened the world's eyes. This man was known as Charles Darwin.

Charles Darwin was a British naturalist and geologist, looking over his book: **The Origins of Species** briefly, many viewed Darwin as someone who believed men evolved from monkeys. As I challenge many of my peers and those I seek to inspire, I always promote the need to dig deeper into any subject. Let's begin to dig up the nature of the organism and the nature of the condition. Darwin insisted that "organic beings must be exposed during several generations to new conditions." These new conditions could cause a great amount of variation, he stated that "once it begins to vary it generally continues to vary for many generations"[1]

So what exactly does this mean to life? What he is stating is that the nature of the organism within a certain condition will need to vary in order to adapt or survive in that condition. In life we (the organism) must transpire into variety; adapting to a given situation (our condition). In his studies, the organism's variations varied for many generations. In our world we learn to adapt and then teach; generation after generation learning to adapt from the previous generation, is that not the same? Let's continue to dig. Throughout this book we cover the history of our lives, the salvation, the love, the disappointment, and the growth, the history of society, our perceived nature and the understanding of life itself.

Species vary, not all birds share the same purpose or look. Their need to survive is based on what type of bird they are and their condition/environment. We all experience life differently based on our situation, in this aspect we adapt in order to survive. This was one of Darwin's theories that have influenced my poetry themed around life. So in these aspects evolution serves to be true. Now here's the dispute. Aligning my beliefs with Darwin's, we all evolve, but evolution to me is not what we typically perceive it to be. Take a plant and cross-breed it with another and you would form a new species of plants. The original form of the two plants fused together to create a new life form, that's evolution. A mother and a father creating a baby is simply evolution. We grow from being a "seed" to a newborn, a newborn to a child and finally a man; the point of evolution that I bring up in attempting to answer the question of what is life, is to bring awareness of life's cycles.

We see that we all evolve, which means we can all grow into something great. We see that we all can adapt given our conditions. We see that evolution within ourselves is life. No? Still not catching your eye? Well let's dig deeper.

Life's Changes

Symbolism is something a lot of great philosophers, leaders, organizations, religions, cultures, activists, poets, musicians, you name it; all use symbolism to exhort meaning. So what is life? If evolution didn't capture an understanding for you then we will replace the word evolution with transpiring. Transpiring is defined as something happening or occurring. In this moment of something happening, something else is affected. Some may call this the butterfly effect. Whoa! Butterflies, isn't that part of the title within this book? Yes, butterflies share a correlation with life itself. In explaining the metamorphosis of butterflies and their connection to evolution we then use this symbolism to answer questions surrounding life cycles.

Many cultures believe that butterflies represent change, development, beauty and hope. Similar to us butterflies begin their passage into their lives as eggs, once hatched they live the beginning of their lives as larva (caterpillars). Throughout this stage of their lives they shed, feed and adapt. Shedding signifies the lost of their former selves, beginning anew. They also start to grow their wings in this stage and right before the pupa stage their wings are fully attached. Then they form a chrysalis or as we all call it a cocoon. In this stage, their cells are reforming themselves to completely change the larva. Something is happening, something is occurring; transpiring. Once hatched from the cocoon they are full of color and beauty, able to fly once their wings are dry and fully expanded.

Now correlate a butterfly with human life. We start off as a small fetus and grow into a newborn baby. In this stage of our lives we are nurtured, taught; we feed, and we learn. As a child we have the capabilities to start seeking out who and what we are in life, just like the caterpillars. We change, they shed. We start to see our aspirations, role-models, dreams and we are ready and eager to spread our wings. So right before we get to our chrysalis stage something begins to happen, something begins to occur, our paths are somewhat set just as to their wings being fully intact. From teenagers to adults in life we experience complete change, complete metamorphosis. Though we do not undergo a complete change in appearance like a caterpillar to a butterfly, we do change in how we view ourselves. Take a moment and look into the mirror. See any difference? From a week before until now you can't notice the slightest of difference in your appearance. That doesn't mean you haven't changed. Your mental state, your aspirations, even your goals change a little. When reminiscing over your childhood you have changed and came a long way, in this aspect you have undergone metamorphosis.

Andrew Burgess writes that an engraver named William Blake remarked that "as in art as in life, the decisive factor is how you draw a line."[2] In answering what is life, how evolution and metamorphosis connects to life; we are designed to follow lines. Cross certain lines and life could become ominous. Live life without lines and then we'll find ourselves asking the same questions I asked earlier in this introduction: "what if life had no end and death is a mere myth?" These lines that we create in our lives motivate the need to debate the existence of life of itself.

This is the debate of life, butterflies being life's cycles; debates being the argument, thus the argument of butterflies.

"Where the messenger left off"

The importance of the number 33

Picture if you will, numbers flying all over. Instead of seeing a flower we see the number of atoms that makes up that flower or when you stare in the mirror you see the number of cells within yourself. To me 33 is more than just a number. It is symbolic in many ways. In science the number 33 represents arsenic and it's used mainly to strengthen alloys in copper and also lead. Think of a car battery (lead-acid) we can have the oil and the engine but without the power from the battery the car moves nowhere.

Small doses of arsenic can be in the water we drink or the air we breathe. To me that is symbolic of the number 33 being all around us.

33 can also be a religious reference. Some believe that Jesus Christ died at the age of thirty-three where he left the gospels of the new testaments to his disciples to spread to the nations.

"By the age of 33 I will leave my message where the messenger left off though I pray he forgives me for my blasphemy."

That is a quote that is dear to my mind, body and soul, for it means that my poetry and my philosophies are my message and that by the age of when our savior died I too will inspire and leave my work and legacy behind. 33 is my symbol; my message as it is written. In the world of Free-Masons, 33 is the highest degree a mason can accomplish. As you can see the number 33 plagues my mind, I always believed that my poetry and message come from within.

A collection of my poetry is inspired by contemporary poetry, spoken word, traditional verse as well as free verse. So I challenge my reader this one task. Take if you will a shovel and step outside and begin to dig. The moment that shovel hits the ground and disrupts its surface you are considered to be digging beneath the surface. So now, picture your mind as the shovel, and instead of digging up the earth I allow you the opportunity to dig beneath my poetry.

Understanding my verse is one thing, but I challenge you guys to read the review and dig deeper. As a poet all I ever wanted was to write a piece of art that simply sung with a beautiful voice. That voice resonating with the harmony of my message. The reviews you will find throughout this book are my interpretation of these poems. Though I wrote the poems and the review, I still challenge my readers to form your own interpretation of the poems as they relate to you all.

Many authors and philosophers have inspired my poetry throughout the years: Ali Shariati, Frantz Fanon and Robert Herrick are the main three that have influenced me the most.

Enjoy.

The Devil's Narrative

Four Part Poem Series

Death of Innocence

Abomination, staring into the mirror looking at mankind's painted picture,

I can only cry out death to the virgins.

For passing time soon the shadows lead,

And the children will follow.

Reaching for the light that the darkness will swallow.

The guilt of the boy lies heavily on the lamb.

It's lost and the wolf doesn't sleep.

The truth is never heard so the wolf feasts on the sheep, continuously.

Sins of the blood stained the knife that has pierced men's soul.

Tearing them from their salvation I can only cry out death of innocence.

A Sinner's Plague

To the sick hour of this pestilent day.

The more songs and praise to the heavenly gates,

Darkened and twisted the crusades.

As their beliefs plunged swords into men,

Sending them to rest in the immortals torture chambers.

As they murdered their virtues while embracing their sins,

Knocking on Sheol's door*.

As smoke choked the Everglades,

Blinding the flocks and poisoning the seas.

Plague ruined Western Europe.

As each field was filled with blood,

Scientists thought to rebel.

For they were the first to go against any church,

Blasphemers they were.

Preparing for battle,

Though the burden of war destroyed them all.

Leaving only a feast for vultures and mites,

To dance and prickle,

Through mornings and nights.

Inspirational Orbs

The absence of visible light.

Those rivers that flow of fire and ice.

Frowns from the cold hearted,

Soon becoming dark angels living on the turtle's back.*

Born of Eve,

Taken care of by Temeluchus* the merciless angel who chokes the damned.

He plants the seeds of torment which grows those tall creepy trees,

Acting as a solar eclipse.

But here comes inspirational orbs which can change the deep conscious,

Influencing mental processing, subliminal.

Changing individuals,

Floating in the dark giving visuals,

To the now visible, light.

(Light up the darkness)

The Devil's Opera

Every inch of earth and water the dead does slumber,

And soon all men will become their interred cohorts.

To whomever has had a veil over his eyes and darkness in his soul,

I will raise thee and he shall worship me as his Deity.

To whomever refuses,

I will remember him as the one, who has heard and sung of my orchestras,

And I will show his soul no remorse.

So cometh, take up this sword as I give chance, and kill me.

End of Series

Devil's Narrative Review

"I will remember him as the one, who has heard and sung of my orchestras"

The series open with **"*The Death of Innocence,*"** the Devil himself narrating each poem. His plan is to help mankind realize his own destruction. He uses **"*The Death of Innocence"*** as his driving tool. *"Abomination, staring into the mirror looking at mankind's painted pictures"* describes what has already transpired. Mankind's painted pictures are left in ruin, left in chaos, left as an abomination. In each stanza he describes some sort of purity being destroyed. The virgins, the children and the lamb are all symbolic of innocence. His opening poem allows the readers to see for themselves how we as men destroy our own innocence thus aiding the Devil in his plan. In the first stanza the virgins are left in this chaotic world (man's painted picture). So when it's time to raise their children or birth them in the second stanza they no longer have their purity to offer, *"The roots reaching for the lights that the darkness will swallow."* There's no hope for the child raised in a world that continues to be an abomination that continues to be dark. That's when the Devil thrives on the children, he uses them to feed on the last innocence that is left; the lamb. In many religions

particularly Christianity the lamb is seen as The
Christ or The Messiah. The feud between God and the
Devil is then mentioned in the third stanza. The
children no longer hold their innocence and the
virgins are far gone that the Devil sees hope in the
children to destroy the last hope for men; his attempt
to destroy what The Messiah represents. As a child I
was raised into believing that lying is bad. So my
mother, teachers, mentors would always tell the story
about *The Boy Who Cried Wolf.* For those who don't
know the story a quick summary of it is that a young
boy was given the responsibility of being a sheep-
keeper. One day for his amusement the boy cried wolf
and the villagers would rush down to help though no
wolf was there. Again the child did the same and the
same result; the villagers would come to help, yet still
no wolf. As they say third time's the charm, well not
for this young boy. A wolf actually appeared and
when the boy cried wolf the villagers was on to his
games and never showed. The wolf was left to feast
on all the sheep. In the third stanza the Devil realizes
the power in deception, so as the children continue to
lie the lamb is left to suffer. Leaving only but sin in a
world of guilt, *"sins of the blood stained the knife
that has pierced men's soul, tearing them from their
salvation I can only cry out death of innocence."*

To further his argument, Lucifer thinks back
to a story where sin, deception and chaos destroyed a

region. **"A Sinner's Plague"** serves as his example. Keep in mind that Lucifer is narrating each poem, so as he speaks *"to the sick hour of this pestilent day"* he is describing a time that he can remember walking the earth.

> *"The more songs and praise to the heavenly gates*
>
> *Darkened and twisted the crusades"*

The reign of The Crusades and The Christian Church weighed heavy towards Lucifer's perception of sin. What he is stating in the quote above is that the more the crusades fought for the Priest and the Church, the more they killed, they became darker than, and equally as evil as we perceive the Devil to be. The Crusades in their own mind were the protagonist of the poem later turned antagonist. This fact is important in understanding the narrative of Lucifer. He was the morning star, the most beautiful angel Heaven has ever seen. He later rebelled against God, now fallen to live in the depths of hell reeking of his own sin. The crusades serve as something he can relate to. He understands the great intentions they have yet he is intimate with the evil and chaos they cause. The ultimate sin of letting go of their virtues only to embrace what is wrong is why he tells this particular story. The message following **"The Death of Innocence"** of what sin and guilt really is. In

November 1095, Pope Urban II called the Crusades to liberate The Church of God in Jerusalem.[3] Jonathan Phillips's studies on the crusades stated that "Urban was responsible for the spiritual well-being of his flock and the crusade presented an opportunity for the sinful knights of western Europe to cease their endless in-fighting and exploitation of the weak (lay people and churchmen alike) and to make good their violent lives. Urban saw the campaign as a chance for knights to direct their energies towards what was seen as a spiritually meritorious act."[3] this influence later caused the earlier Crusades to attack Muslims and other men/groups that they felt were against the Christian Church. Lucifer then takes this opportunity to introduce another group that has been overlooked whenever discussions of The Crusades came about; Scientist.

"Sending them to rest in the immortals torture chambers

As they murdered their virtues while embracing their sins

Knocking on Sheol's door"

As Lucifer continues to relate to the crusades, he believes that with each murdering act they commit they send the men they kill to hell. (The immortals torture chambers) This plague of war started to ruin the land. While the crusades sought out those who opposed The Church; scientist were preparing to fight back. In a book titled **Angels and Demons** by Dan Brown; he had a different take on the "so called" Illuminati. His book described them as early scientist who believed in science over God. Well the story goes that once The Catholic Church killed off a few scientists, the remaining members formed a secret society to retaliate against The Church.[4] In *"A Sinner's Plague"* I use this creative thriller to implement it into my poetry. The war between these scientist and Crusades; to start off as a battle between religious beliefs and free will of believing in one's ability to understand science caused this terror of blood spill. This story serves as The Devil's reasoning as to why he receives the blame for the horrors within the world. He opens his narrative by describing the loss of innocence, followed by the story of Priest and Popes using religion as a tool for murder, that murder being the loss of innocence. All hope is lost, we could easily assume, but his narrative is far from over.

"The absence of visible light

Those rivers that flow of fire and ice

Frowns from the cold hearted"

Home, a place we all can describe. Whether we love our homes or not, we know it: from the corners to the ceiling and even the spots that may creep as we walk over them. Darkness; being the absence of visible light and the rivers of fire and ice, these are descriptions of Lucifer's home. A place where there are only frowns and cold hearts. In keeping with his themes of losing innocence, he explains that we are now dark angels roaming the earth or as I stated *"the turtle's back."* Going back to when the children and virgins lost their innocence we all are born from woman; Eve being the first woman to walk earth in Christian belief, found in the book of Genesis; believed to the beginning of birth. *"Born of Eve"* we all are born through woman, The Devil himself cannot oversee everything mapped out in his plot/narrative. He hires his chief tormenter Temeluchus to be the care-taker and overseer of children, born into the world raised by sin. Planting the seeds for children to grow into their transgression causes the world to be dark as if it was covered by a solar eclipse.

So is all hope lost by this point? Lucifer knows his stand in this continuous battle of good versus evil. To answer is all hope lost, he explains that there are inspirational orbs, people that remained virtuous throughout all of this guilt and transgression. Ones that could change the deep conscience to influence others individually by changing their mental state; these innocent men and woman are able to seek out the darkness and change someone in hope that they also spread the light, creating an army of "orbs" to light up the darkness.

By this point in his narrative, Lucifer has explained the loss of innocence, gave a story describing that loss, and even gave us hope as to how we can take back our innocence.

"To whomever has had a veil over his eyes and darkness in his soul, I will raise thee and he shall worship me as his deity"

This is the Lucifer we know and understand. Not the one speaking of human flaw and giving hope, but the one who seeks out revenge and destruction. Whoever stayed in his darkness refusing to live in the light, the devil will raise them up to become one with his army/demons. His opera as we read in **"The Devil's Opera"** is simply his music and his plan to use this darkness that we created as man to destroy us. In the end whoever refuses to be a part of that plan in his attempts to destroy the orbs he states that "*I will remember he as the one who has sung and heard of my orchestra and shall show his soul no remorse.*" Lucifer isn't planning on the hope we found in **"Inspirational orbs"** to come about. He plans to hurt those that does not come a board with his ideals. He gives one final chance for us to take up our 'swords' to stop him, to end this darkness that we continue to live in, because if we don't end it, then he will continue to reign over us with his darkness.

End of Review

Shinigami November 13th

Beside my bed where I lay at night.

There's a haunting soul that sits in fright.

He never speaks he only watch.

As I sleep I feel his touch.

He comes from corners where it's dark,

Some nights he's there, some nights he's not.

His name to me? I call him Grim.

For when I sleep, I think of him.

Will he kill or just there to scare?

I don't know but whenever I'm awake, he's never there.

Is he a guardian or is he death?

Tonight I close my eyes,

On this night I lost my breath.

Shinigami November 13th Review

Shinigami* *"On this night I lost my breath"*

I would never forget the cold chills of November 13th. That whole day I felt something or someone shadowing my every move. I was in the small city of Dongducheon, South Korea. On this day the mist and fog from the mountains covered the morning skies holding the sun hostage. Normally I went about my day cheerfully, always upbeat, but at this point nothing seemed right.

Something slowed me down, like I was carrying a sled weighing a ton. I felt drained like every ounce of fluids in my body streamed into the crappy drainage system. My blood seemed to be the coldest and my tongue became so dry that I would cut the corners of my lips whenever I tried to moisten them. I became distant from others, my friends trying to converse with me going about their daily lives. My mind wasn't there that day, I was lost walking throughout the day but all I saw was darkness. "Was this shadow protecting me or haunting me?" I began to ask. I couldn't make out a face nor was the structure of the shadow fully intact. I mean I saw what appeared to be arms and legs, but it was too blurry to make out.

Then there's night fall, and its beginning to get closer to a nights rest. That's when I see him. No longer blurry, fully intact, but still no face. This wasn't the first time he has came by my bed side and it seems only when I'm in bed is when he shows himself fully. Throughout the days he's only a chill to my spine, but on nights like these he's actually there. No light could escape how dark he was. He was darker than any black hole. Paralyzed I became. I couldn't move as he haunted me, moving from the corners of my room to the foot of my bed. I knew then that he wasn't here to protect me. An angel wouldn't paralyze me and then frolic around taunting me.

Many psychiatrists would say that I was simply having a lucid dream. Where I believe I'm consciously awoke but still asleep. I assure you this was not the case. Grim I began to call him, pleading and begging to see another day. My chest became heavy; I started to realize that the ton I was carrying earlier was only my heart weighing the burden of this fright. It's very hard to breathe when you are paralyzed and feel as though your life is almost over.

I closed my eyes; prayer I thought could save me. "Grim! I ask of you to let me live again." I exhaled slowly, trying to savor the breath of life. For when it was all over and he took that breath from me. All I could hear was him singing:

"Ring around the rosie, pocket full of posies, ashes ashes, we all fall down"

My surroundings mirrored an underground world, far from where my room was. I saw pale men grasping for medication, though ointment couldn't heal their burns. I saw their eyes full of despair and regret. Women were chained and stretched out on wheel crosses, but they no longer had wombs; that wretched song still playing in the background as I began to sink in the same despair that the others around me were in. I looked up to see Grim finally with a face smiling at me as if he won a prize.

He introduced me to a man that demanded power as he walked through this dark place. Every soul stood still, afraid of his presence. The few words he spurred at me were:

"I come from the crossroads, where my mother has spent, most of her years singing and playing music. She waged to a man who offered her gold, if she traded her womb and most of her soul. She hesitated but she lusted for greed, so she let this man lay with her as he planted his seed. She later gave birth in the center where these roads connect, her soul so far gone into the darkest of depths. She

stole from me the nourishment of a mother and gave me nothing, nothing but a name. The only thing I hold dear so call me Damian.

He then gave Grim a blood contract for me to sign, for my message to be highlighted in gold. I refused boldly telling him no. I suffered his stare as it haunts me till this day, but I'm grateful I was able to awake on November 14th.

The Elephant That Sat by the Door

If you had to cut open my body and tell me what you would find,

Would you find a belly full of swine?

Or even a poisoned boy?

See, life is but an elephant that sat by the door.

Superstitions,

Throwing salt over my shoulders.

Never splitting poles,

For I never knew if Jehovah,

Had many blessings.

Because it seems that life is full of curses.

Swaying away from the narrow path that few men find,

For I never felt like that path was ever worth it.

All because of four years of bad luck and many curses.

See, the moon doesn't guide a man to safety,

It only helps him hide.

But I once knew a man lying in the alley way,

Where the moon-light shined.

And I wonder if he ever broke mirrors or even fulfilled his only purpose.

See my train of thought got me feeling like I'm trapped,

Like I've been fighting so many wars.

And I've been sinning for so long,

That it seems like my mindset is locked down in Sheol.

Wondering would I ever get a taste of Abraham's bosom?

Or will I forever fulfill the belly of the beast?

So God please come down and cast out this demon inside me.

See that's my only excuse for why I'm having all this bad luck,

And my only preference was simply a blessing.

So I find myself throwing salt over my shoulders,

Never splitting poles never breaking mirrors and never walking under ladders.

And I will always open up the umbrella outside of the building,

For whenever the rain did shatter.

Just to be cautious,

But not once as I recall, not once as I recall,

Ever falling to my knees and saying a prayer to the Lord.

Because I always believed that the elephant sat by the door.

The Elephant That Sat by the Door Review

I come from a small town in the peninsula area of Virginia; Smithfield. As far as I can remember back I asked my mother why she always had a statue elephant facing the door. I went to my aunt's house and there I saw it again, the same with my grandmother. It amused me because the other statues were facing towards the living room. The angels, the statue of Christ, even the small collectable dogs were all facing the same direction. But the elephant in every home in my family were all facing away towards the door.

She finally explained to me that the elephant facing the door represents good-luck for your household/ good luck for your home. Many superstitious business owners would place elephants by their building doors to bring in good fortune. The elephant represents protection, stability and strength. The idea of having the elephant facing the door is to bring in any good fortune, great protection, wisdom and strength before entering your home.

"If you were to cut open my body and tell me what you would find, would you find a belly full of swine or even a poisoned boy?"

My body is my temple, it is my home. Throughout this poem my actions in trying to bring good luck into my life is physically and spiritually symbolic of the elephant. I cleansed myself of eating pork (swine) many years ago. I decided to open this poem by stating as if my body was toxic and in a dire need to be clean. Life is like the elephant that sat by the door. In order to come about this good fortune I needed to find superstitious ways to bring about this luck and cleanse that I sought out.

"Throwing salt over my shoulders, never splitting poles for I never knew if Jehovah…"

Spiritually we pray and pray and pray in hopes that our life leaps off into success. I, looking to be cleansed of not only the affects swine has on the body but the toxic it represent in life. Thus putting emphasis on "a poisoned boy" in Matthew chapter 8 verse 31: demons begged Jesus that if he was to cast them out then he should send them into a herd of pigs.

"So the devils besought him, saying, if thou cast us out, suffer us to go away into the herd of swine."
Matthew 8:31[5]

So you see this representation of poison, this marked home of mine which is my mind, body and soul has to be preset. *"I never knew if Jehovah had many blessings, swaying away from the narrow path few men find for I never felt the path to be worth it."* Going back to bible references

"Enter ye in at the strait gate: for wide is the gate, and broad is the way, that leadeth to destruction, and many there be which go in thereat" Matthew 7:13[6]

I have found the narrow (strait) gate/path that few men find. But due to many years of bad luck my anger and disappointment I decided to ignore that path and take the wide broad way/path towards destruction.

"The moon doesn't guide a man to safety it only helps him hide, but I once knew a man lying in the alley way where the moon-light shined."

Even in our darkest nights we could still hide under the moon's light. Its powerful glow that encases everything we believe is right. I once knew a homeless man comforted by the moon. The alley way was his home though he lacked the protection of doors. Unfortunately there was no place for elephants in his world; nowhere to even put them if he believed in its good-fortune. Was it too late for him? I began to ask myself. Was it the lack of superstition that caused this man to be down on his luck, living in alleyways? My mind became flooded, left to believe that a mirror cracked was this man's ultimate "down fall." First my body, now my mind is poisoned; Trapped into a belief of superstitions that cripples forward thinking. My beliefs are tangled, stuck between faith in the Lord and luck remedies. This back and forth creates a war within me causing my mind to seem locked away in Sheol.

Abraham's Bosom*

Luke 16: 19-31[7]

In a discomforted place spiritually, my mind is plagued, remaining in the depths of Sheol. This is figuratively speaking for I find myself lost. To better understand the reference of Abraham's bosom we turn again to the divine word of The Holy Bible. There was a story found in the bible of a beggar man named Lazarus, he laid at the gate of a rich man. The rich man was clothed with fine purple linen and he fared at things that were expensive and great looking. Lazarus desired to be fed crumbs that fell from the rich man's table, even having the dogs come to lick his body full of sores. Lazarus the beggar died and the angels carried him to be by Abraham's side (Abraham's bosom). The rich man also died and was buried. The rich man now in hell (Sheol, Hades) looks up at a far sees Abraham and Lazarus. He begs to Abraham the father of righteous men to allow Lazarus to dip his finger in water to cool off his tongue, for he is tormented in the flames. Abraham reminded the rich man of his life and good things he received and the evil things Lazarus received.

"And besides all this, between us and you there is a
great gulf fixed: so that they which would pass from
hench to you cannot; neither can they pass to us, that
would come from thence" Luke 16:26[8]

Now neither knowing that there is nothing
Lazarus nor Abraham could do to save him the rich
man begs Abraham to send Lazarus to save and warn
his five brothers of this tortuous torment.

The fate of the rich man was torment forever,
and his brothers would most likely face the same fate
for not repenting. Abraham told the rich man that his
brothers have Moses and the prophets to hear, he
rebuttals by stating that they will not hear the
prophets. Send Lazarus from the dead to convince
them, but surly Abraham responds by stating even the
dead can't save them if they can't hear Moses. *"Will I
forever fulfill the belly of the beast?"* Will I face the
same fate as the rich man? Is the man in the alley way
Lazarus? These unanswered questions trouble me.

My only hope is to ask God to cast demons
away from me and send them into a herd of pigs, as
we read before. I continue to remain superstitious,
throwing salt over my shoulders, never splitting
poles, never breaking mirrors, never walking under
ladders and always opening the umbrellas outside of
buildings. But never has it crossed my mind to just
fall to my knees and let the God of Abraham become

my good-fortune. Because in my temple, my home, my mind body and soul, I've always believed that the elephant sat by the door.

The Day That Hope Killed

See the day that hope killed.

Was the day my mind went insane,

because if it's all the same it came,

Like a thief in the night.

And if I'm not mistaken, It appeared to be a phoenix.

Rising from the ashes the hope that I was dreaming.

It sought me as its victim.

A man with all the potential and too much ambition.

Then it took the form of a woman.

That lovely walk and beautiful shape.

I couldn't help but only listen.

So to the beauty of her remarks and power of a smile.

She looked me dead in my eyes and used her favorite

lines. Which were,

"Boy oh boy, you still have time"

Not realizing it was only lies,

So I fell for her deceit.

Weaken by defeat,

Just give me a pen and paper so I can write the

headlines as they read.

"The Lord has the righteous living poor, living poor,

and living poor"

So now I'm searching for greed,

But she say remain patient for patience is a virtue,

but I'm sinful than all.

Like lusting for more proud to be a man while having

dreams as a boy.

See I gave carbon dioxide for all the oxygen I

breathe.

Just like I done gave hope all my damn dreams.

So now I'm stuck.

Going back to the basics,

Drinking in moderation, but moderation leads to me

being wasted. Blacked out awakening moments later

contemplating. Darkening thoughts like suicide, how

could I face this?

Cursing the Lord's name in vain,

But I'm not trying to be no atheist.

So now I'm stuck writing rhymes,

Flipping pages and flipping pages and

Trying to write my own bible to justify my own ways.

See hope done murdered men and stole dreams since

the moment of her creation and now all those smiles

are ancient.

So when it was time to talk to Lucifer.

He offered me the materials and gold,

And I had to tell him no, because hope done made me

many promises.

He chuckled and he laughed and said,

"Can't you see, that I created hope to define the fine

meanings of religion. So that man can say he's

counting blessings while putting a hold on his dreams

and aspirations. Only so that my plans can be

conceived. Like Adam and Eve to the forbidden tree I

brought death into this world. So you mean to tell me,

that you're patiently waiting on your dreams while

dying believing in hope. Ah please! If you were even smart you'll find hope and take back all your dreams, but you won't, because you're so heavily into your faith that you believe if you wait then hope will come around and try to meet you face to face."

That's when it hit me.

It wasn't Lucifer that was speaking,

but more so of my conscience that give me these words.

See my heart is torn so that's why I view hope as a girl.

I'm a man that's wants it all.

So I stopped putting my trust in hope and put my trust into the Lord.

See the day that hope killed

is the day that God will,

Stand up and make us stronger and he'll soon reveal.

That we had to go through this struggling journey.

So when hope comes around we'll finally have a

testimony.

And she'll pull from her bag and take the form of

reality.

Giving us back our dreams so we could live life

happily.

Religions at War

Allahu Akbar! Allahu Akbar! Hallelujah!

See these are the different ways on how to praise God

Though it may change through the mouths of religion

We all feel as we can see it and we know that we can sense it

Omitting to the fact that religions are the same

But how we praise God makes the difference

Like, Allahu Akbar! Allahu Akbar! Hallelujah!

One meaning all praises due to Allah

And the other meaning God to be praised

See don't you get my drift of how it all sounds the same?

But we are so stuck into our ways

That we forget about our faith and we tend to separate

And only following our traditions

And yes many cultures lead to diversity but religion only leads to division.

For instance,

You have Christians going against Christians

Because the Jehovah witness don't like the Baptist

And the Baptist don't like the other denominations

And denominations against the Catholics

Even to the point where the Jews only read from the
Old Testament

Because they can't believe that Jesus Christ was a
bastard.

Having a stepfather Joseph to come in and raise the
Son of God

Oh my! That is blasphemous!

Not realizing that Jesus was a Jew and also the King
of Nazareth.

So they crucified Him but he resurrected after

And I'm a firm believer in forgiveness

But I also read that you should reap what you sow

So is it safe to say that when the Holocaust came around

We shouldn't really weep for the Jew?

Oh forgive me for being blunt or even blatant

But the Jews that I speak of come from the Synagogues of Satan

Damn that's got me sounding racist

But basically I'm just trying to be free

Of this curse that you can read about in Deuteronomy

So therefore I'll let history speak

And the purpose of this poem is to let history reach

Into the minds and the eyes

To help man realize

That he's forgotten about his faith

But focused more on his religion

See God made man into his own image

So what did man do?

He took his own culture and made God into his own vision

Allahu Akbar! Allahu Akbar! Hallelujah!

All praises due to whom?

Because some will say that wherever you're from

Then your God is going to look like you

So that's why Buddha looks Asian

And some say God is Caucasian

And some say God comes from a high caves

And Jesus Christ looks white

So can you really blame white supremacy for having a black slave?

And would you say that my savior is Caesar Borgia?

But to my rebuttal I am a descendant from Abraham

Jacob and Isaac born of Israel

Nationality of my origins

But now my land is only full of war and plague

They are crying out dooms day for the days are damned

So I look over to my brother for keeps

As he's crying out Assalamu Alaikum, deceit

So I try to turn the other cheek

For I don't see any peace

From Genesis to Revelations

See these pages are torn

For I don't see any faith anymore

For we all have fallen victim to religions at war. We all have fell victim to religions at war.

Religions at War Review

"We all have fell victim to religions at war"

Through every battle and every war, there has been a great divide. The Union against the Confederate South, Japan evading China, allies against allies in the immense calamity of the World Wars. This divide has left millions in ruin, has left many to rest secluded with only one mind. The same as faith being disputed by religion, religion being fought by belief, belief being misguided, directed towards war. In this review we will discuss the uncertainty of religion pinned against another religion, the abstraction of a goal; that goal being salvation over which religion is right.

What happens when there is a divide, is simple, everyone involved is separated. Maybe not separate physically, for we know that we coexist with others who have dissimilar views and religious beliefs, but in the sense that we are separated spiritually and mentally. It has become a norm to remote yourself from those who believe in a different way. This different chain of thought seems to be harmless until that infinite uncertain goal begins to teach. For instance Christians will disagree with Israelites, even though they share common beliefs and read from the same text valued as divinity. The goal sought out by modern Christians is to gather followers to be Christ-like, to repent, to accept Jesus as their lord and savior. That same goal is sought out by the black conscience-movement know as the

Israelites. The only difference is how they go about teaching that goal, attempting to prove who is right and what is wrong. These beliefs, once harmless, now creates a divide for the attempts of reaching said goal. This causes religions to be at war.

> *"We all feel as we can see it and we know that we can sense it*
>
> *Omitting to the fact that religions are the same*
>
> *But how we praise God makes the difference"*

As I stated before and throughout the rest of this review I would try to persuade you into believing that religions are the same, hanging loosely onto the word 'believing.' While I do agree that your difference in belief carries an enormous amount of significance, I am here to help you realize that religion causes us to divide ignoring the faith and belief that was once the foundation of our/your religion to begin with. So with that being said we omit to the fact that religions are the same. They are the same in terms of three things: motives, history and a supreme being versus an iniquity.

Let's talk about the first term, motives. In majority of the world's religions, including the most popular ones like the Nation of Islam, Christianity, Buddhism, Hinduism, and Judaism, all have a similar motive. That motive being to achieve salvation through faith and worship, whether that salvation is through reincarnation or a higher paradise, the motive to get there through your deeds here on earth and your surrender to a higher being is then the focus of the teaching, thus creating similar motives.

Next is the history of creation. The Qur'an and the Holy Bible are very parallel in terms of speaking about creation, the heavens and the earth both being constructed by the most high. Most religions share a creation story, a history of how the earth and man came to be. As a child I can recall of a native tribe, unaware of their name now, their mythical story of how earth was created.

The story like many other creation stories started with an abyss of complete darkness. A bird flying throughout this abyss being symbolic of a deity, flew and flew unable to land and rest, the bird continued to fly. It flew until it saw a turtle's back. The turtle swimming in the water, the bird landed to rest forever grateful of the turtle, he blessed the turtle to grow. The turtle's back began to grow and this is how land was created, how the earth was formed; the turtle being symbolic of Mother Nature and the bird being a spiritual being that continues to fly watching over the earth (turtle).

Looking into those who practice Buddhism, they do not necessarily believe in a creator, but more so the birth and rebirth in a cyclic law (a cycle of existence).

You see a creation story holds value in the history of any religion, leading to the next term which is a supreme being versus some form of iniquity. In any religion, backed by history and motives, we see that there is a divine good versus a wicked evil, God against Lucifer, Heaven and Hell, evildoers versus good deeds. With these three aspects, religions share similarity so as I write "But how we praise God makes the difference" is then the vocal point of distinguishing between your religion and someone else. That difference being one thing, faith within your religion.

Faith is powered by belief, throughout history religious believers have fought against atheist (non-believers) or that is how it appeared. Ali Shariati writes that this is not the case; the truth is that religions fight against other religions. As I stated before, faith has to be powered by belief, with that belief it is easy to see that non-believers play no significant role in jeopardizing the goal of believers. What I am saying is those atheists do not worry themselves with salvation, they simply don't believe in it, while believers try to teach others of their true fate. The fear of the afterlife does not strike the atheists, that fear is set aside exclusively for believers.

So who is right and who is wrong? That question when speaking religion rules out the atheist. Why? Under the teachings of Ali Shariati; he gives a lecture on *Religion vs. Religion*. He speaks of history, the earliest documentation given to man being older than 20 to 40 thousand years old. This history through geology, myths, field-archeology and legends has shown religion all throughout [2.] What this details is the proof that religion in some form has been with man in his earliest civilizations. Up until now religion has always went up against other religions, whether it be monotheism, paganism, and polytheism never seeming to face atheistic.

"Like, Allahu Akbar! Allahu Akbar! Hallelujah!

One meaning all praises due to Allah

And the other meaning God to be praised

See don't you get my drift of how it all sounds the same?"

So let's get to the war, let's make sense of this divide. The Nation of Islam and Christianity, as stated before, share common similarities. The meaning to praise may differ depending on the tongue but the meaning remains the same. Black churches particularly in America have members that may raise their hands high to praise screaming the phrase Hallelujah. Muslims choose to say Allahu Akbar to praise their god. This part of the poem, though brief and direct, is used to describe the common theme with religions. So in answering who is right and who is wrong, the dispute would never end. Some may shout "All praises due to Allah" rebuttal by "All praises due to God" or "NO! All praises due to Yahweh." So you see who is right and who is wrong depends on the opposing religion. This one question has been the focus creating this divide and causing many of its followers to lose sight of the faith behind the religion.

We are stuck in our own ways forgetting faith and only focusing on our religion. This world adds diversity by presenting to us many cultures and traditions. It is easier for us to grasp another culture to experience different traditions, but it is harder for one to convert to another religion. Reason why is the fear of being wrong, fear of losing what you believed to be right in order to gain another perspective on spirituality. If the Baptist is wrong and has only worshipped God, then his spirituality would lie on whoever is right. If he chooses to convert to The Nation of Islam and now worships Allah and it just so happens that the Baptist's perspectives were right then he faces once again his spirituality in terms of salvation. The unknown has always brought upon fear plain and simple. So with that, religion begins to divide.

"Religion only leads to division

For instance you have Christians going against Christians

Because the Jehovah Witness don't like the Baptist

And the Baptist against other denominations

Denominations against the Catholics

Even to the point where the Jews only read from the Old Testament because they can't believe that Jesus Christ was a bastard"

Filter out what you have learned and learn our ways of teaching. That is how denominations of Christianity try to convert followers. Reading the same text and sharing similar views they will still divide themselves amongst each other. Starting to see how religion is the same yet creating division? The purpose of this poem is to build faith behind whatever religion you choose and turn away from the religion itself. I consider myself to be an Israelite, focusing on my faith and beliefs is what brings me understanding and knowledge, if I were to only focus on the religion then I would find myself being like the sheep waiting for someone to guide me, waiting for someone to tell me what I need to know.

This is how the Baptist misunderstands the Jehovah Witness and vice versa, because they allow religion to dictate their faith and guide their belief, instead of allowing their faith and belief to dictate their religion. Looking at this perspective as a whole we see that technically Christianity is the religion. So I ask why the difference or confusion? Starting to get my drift?

The battle is far from over, up until this point we have looked at religion in the sense of three aspects; compared Christianity to its denominations creating division. We have seen that religion has always been with man ruling out the atheist in this war, so let's continue to dig.

In Judaism we begin to see a vast gap between Christianity. So as I write the beliefs followed by a Jew,

"Having a step father Joseph to come in and raise the son of god oh my! That is blasphemous"

We then get into what I call the cataclysm of religion. Christ was "prosecuted" if you will by the Jewish people, later sentenced by the Roman Polite to be crucified. As we see in my poem these ideals bring out war-like beliefs; hatred, like,

"I'm a firm believer in forgiveness, but I also read that you should reap what you sow

So is it safe to say,

That when the holocaust came around we shouldn't really weep for the Jew?"

So you see this divide, this war, this misunderstanding only escalates. Placing myself in a realm where I share no sympathy for the Jews. I am left to place blame on them for the genocide and abuse they suffered during the holocaust; viewing them as being from the synagogues of Satan. Religion in this form is now creating racism. That word racism being the cause of control over slaves, it created division amongst people, and brought hatred into the world.

"I'm just trying to be free of this curse that you can read about in Deuteronomy"

This curse that details the experience of the black African American's history in America, found in the book of Deuteronomy. As we continue down this road of hatred and racism we continue to distance ourselves further and further away from faith by using religion. This poem is used to help us realize that. God's image is thus created by man and not the other way around that we have come to believe. Is this right? I'm sure that there are many reasons to dispute it, but the fact that man has divided himself so far from others outside his religion, God's image can now change.

"All praises due to whom?

Because wherever you're from

Then your God is going to look like you."

For instance as I write that Jesus looks white I ask the question: can you blame white supremacy for having the black slave? This is to continue with examples of how religion fuels racism and hatred instead of just relying on faith. To my rebuttal towards Caesar Borgia being my savior, I speak of my origin through my beliefs; Borgia being the common image of Christ.

So as I close this poem covering the divide amongst similarity within Christianity, the aspects of religion in a sense of three terms, the racism and hatred that religion creates and the creation of God's image by man. We then see how religion creates war.

"So I look over to my brother for keeps

As he's crying out Assalamu Alaikum, deceit

So I try to turn the other cheek

For I don't see any peace

From Genesis to Revelations

See these pages are torn

For I don't see any faith anymore

For we all have fallen victim to religions at war. We all have fell victim to religions at war."

Black Sinner

A black sinner

A devil's advocate with no intelligent mind

Just a puppet in society's eyes

When society stereotypes him in this house of lies

Which formed this black man into a black sinner

Like he rather give two quarters for a dime

Which is a hell of a tithe

And instead of finding the beauty in women

He chases the fatter thighs

Which comes no surprise

Just to enter her core and of course its intercourse

Like that's all she's good for

Black sinner

Where art thou black queen?

From Israel to Egypt

You're supposed to be a king

But you're beaten as a slave yet you're stronger than a warrior

Courageous as an activist and leadership of presidents

Black man from the beginning

But now he is only stereotype as eating watermelon and chicken

But that's no bread and butter

So hatred to the starve

Starving leads to the cause

Cause leads to the effect

And effect is now to rob

Robbery is now a job

You do it or you lose it all

Because them pennies aren't enough to them quarters that he lost

See life is but a nightmare sins has a wage

And death is its cost.

Black sinner

This young adolescence

His preference is simply a blessing

A little guidance for he is a fatherless child

Now he's being misguided

Got him saying prayers like

> *Lord forgive me for my sins*
>
> *That I committed last minute*
>
> *It's the day of the serpent*
>
> *And hell on this surface*
>
> *I was chilling with the devil last week*
>
> *And now he's after me and said I owe him some money*
>
> *So dear Lord let me borrow a hundred, couple of dollars*

And I'll pay you back by tomorrow

If not, tell my mother I'm sorry

Because the reaper's coming for me

I'm a black man running

A black sinner

Oh Sweet Wine

Oh sweet wine how smooth you are.

For when time and age is all of beauty.

The sooner I say to seize this drink.

For once grapes have met the rays of the sun.

As age loses it fruitfulness.

Once time succeeds the former, oh that day we know to come.

Oh sweet wine how great we are,

To have shared this life and vine.

Oh Sweet Wine Review

Carpe Diem; seize the opportunity; every moment we are given.

Wine in most cultures is a delicate drink. Some like to enjoy their wine fresh out of the distillery while others wait for it to age to enjoy it then. Whenever we choose to drink our wine we seize every drop, we enjoy its taste, and we compliment it with a meal. In essence we become intimate with its pleasures, the smell, the tartness of it or the sweetness and the color. Certain occasions allow for different variations of wines.

"Oh sweet wine how smooth you are"

If wine is a delicate yet intimate drink, then it's safe to personify wine as women. Giving wine all of her traits and taking every moment with her as value. We compliment our women, we enjoy her taste if you will, and we become stingy with her grace. Think of all the things we do to enjoy wine. We swirl it around in our glass while allowing the aroma to bless our nose. We sip it slowly trying to savor every moment with our wine. So to women we do the same, she takes us away with her grace and we savor the times we share with her. Though some still decide to gulp their wine; either way we pick and choose when or how to enjoy her.

"For when time and age is all of beauty"

Yes when we are young we are at our golden era. We are seen as beautiful, spontaneous and energetic. So while we still share our youth I say to you guys

"Seize this drink."

Soon we will become elders.

"For once grapes has met the rays of the sun, as age loses its fruitfulness"

We all know that grapes turn into raisins once they have been out too long dried up in the sun. Grapes also become elders. Time succeeds to move on, we are merely our former selves, and though left with wisdom and experience we don't have our fruitfulness. We don't contain our youth. So to the sweet wine (female) it was great to have seized the moments we shared in life (the vines I speak of in the last line). Seize the intimate moments we have towards our partners in life.

"Oh sweet swine how great you are, to have shared this life and vine."

The Vow

As the dew sprinkles to the voice of light,

There she cries.

Her warmth is pure like the waters,

Down through the Mississippi river banks.

As the sun peaks over the horizon,

Her comfort blankets the sky.

For in her presence there is heaven.

And when she smiles,

Beauty and all its companions,

Will grace time like an autumn's breeze.

For she is the prettiest thing I've ever seen,

Since I witnessed the rose,

Down by the bayous.

she is the embodiment of perfection.

With a soul so powerful,

She could tide the waters,

Jury the heavens,

And blossom the gardens.

Though she still cries,

Seeking for what I can't understand.

She accepts all of the lesser value.

My angel to whom I'll forever be.

So I vow to dry her cries,

Simply through poetry.

The Vow Review

When writing poetry I was always taught to stay away from abstractions, taught to stay away from speaking love rather than showing love. In this poem, the woman I speak of was so powerful in spirit and in love, that I had no choice but to break that rule.

"As the dew sprinkles to the voice of light

There she cries"

When the morning breaks and as the sky-light begin to hit the grass we notice the morning dew. In this moment I also notice her, crying and all alone. But notice how beautiful she is with a demanding presence when she is around I feel like I'm in heaven. See how powerful she is?

"She could tide the waters

Jury the Heavens,

And blossom the gardens"

But this love is still crying, what could possibly be missing from someone as powerful as this? Trying to answer this question, this is where my "supposed" abstractions come into writing. Her warmth is as pure like the Mississippi river; her presence is comparable to Heaven itself. Her smile has the ability to enchant beauty and all its companions, with the ability to pause and grace time like the leaves floating smoothly through an autumn's breeze.

> *"She is the prettiest thing I've ever seen since I witnessed the rose down by the bayous."*

She is perfection itself or the equivalence of it. Roses don't typically grow in bayous; bayous are mostly marshy outlets. Take a moment and picture a marshy wetland, now imagine a beautiful rose (symbolic of love) growing amongst something deemed not as beautiful. That's how I imagine her, being amongst this world where her beauty stands out so well it's inevitable to not witness her.

> *"Though she still cries"*

This beautiful female of mine, seeking out the wrong men; men of lesser value, men that can take everything she posses spiritually and emotionally and offer her nothing in return; at this point in the poem we see how lovely she is how fond she is how in tuned she is within her power, within her love. Yet she continues to accept lesser value, she is my angel and while she continues to cry, I devise a plan to save her…my poetry.

My poetry encompasses everything she is and wants to be. My poetry is not the poem itself but the feeling within me to express to her that she is this powerful, beautiful, spiritual woman, and the only thing that could save her from her own tears is a man parallel to all of those aspects.

This vow of mines is her safe haven, her template to understanding who she is and her worth, anything less of that would only hurt her creating more tears to follow. So men across the world, let's find our worth so that we could be worthy of women described in this poem.

Her Hips

Her hips carry the ships that sail the hard seas.

Her hips give us aquatic vertebrates so that fisher men can feed.

Her hips give us reasons to breathe.

As Heaven's Lamp awakes and rest in the west,

Passing time her hips continue to twist.

Made from rib, men glazed upon her beauty.

Other than the swift winds, still waters and daffodils across our lands;

Her hips are still considered His greatest creation.

Into the world is given a boy and a girl, and we should cry and accept what her hips give us.

Yet we leap for joy only to ignore refusing to take notice of her flaws.

For she is complicated,

Like the doves built around love, somehow we would still turn to the pigeons.

Sad to say we are ungrateful.

Like the boy who can't appreciate the girl,

But, Oh! How he loves her hips, only to dip in unable to make peace with.

Her hips are wide and also thick but she is sometimes struck with *ka-onde-onde,*

Getting thinner and thinner until she is no more.

And during her ending stages we will see her hips as everything we lived for.

That twist, that shake, that lovely walk that flashes between space and vision.

Because simply her hips are life and every night I slept with her, seizing her prosperous form.

For that body of hers is all that I need.

Her Hips Review

Let's take it back to when Hip-Hop lyricist would break down their lyrics line by line to ensure understanding. I remember going on websites just to read lyrics and then read how the artist broke down those lyrics. It was always cool to me; the excitement behind expanding a verse to mean so much more.

In this review we are going to do just that, we will look at every line and every stanza to fully understand my interpretation of "***Her Hips***." As you guys already know, let's dig.

> *"Her hips carries the ships that sail across the hard seas"*

This opening is so important because it allows me to mold the rest of the poem to follow. Her hips are carrying something; they are carrying the ships that sail the tough hard seas. Two key words in that line were ships and hard. Her hips are carrying hardships. The uncertainty of the sea, the unpredictability of it, its secrets and its dangers are carried by her hips. Life has uncertainties, dangers and also can be unpredictable…it has many secrets. The whales and sea creatures that roam the seas are hidden under a surface; hidden until they show reveal or we go beneath. Life's secrets have to either be revealed or we "go beneath" to seek them out.

> *"Her hips give us aquatic vertebrates so that fishermen can feed"*

Though we may face hardships in return we will have something tangible to show for. Ever went through tough times in life and then somehow, someway, things ease up and life, even if it's brief, throws abundance at you? Once the seas ease up for the fishermen they have fish to eat from; the fish are plentiful, and they are the reward for sticking it through so that the fishermen's families can also feed. Life can be tough, but do not quit, ride out the tough sea to have fish.

"Her hips give us reasons to breathe"

By sticking out the hard seas and not quitting, we have a reason to breathe, a reason to live again. This first stanza opens up the poem to describe life. We go through hardships, we receive reward and we exhale again.

"Her hips carry the ships that sail the hard seas.

Her hips give us aquatic vertebrates so that fisher men can feed.

Her hips give us reasons to breathe.

As Heaven's lamp awakes and rest in the west..."

When I think of paradise, I tend to think of Heaven; the truth and the light being a direct path to paradise. So what is life's light? Life's light is Heaven's lamp, the sun. Focusing on carpe diem and time itself we watch the sun rise and set, from the moment it awakes to the moment it rest, life has gone by.

"Passing time her hips continue to twist"

So with this rise and fall of the sun, time has also moved on. So with the passing of time life continues to move as well. Life may have twists and turns along the way but it never stops nor goes backwards it moves along with time.

"Made from rib, men glazed upon her beauty.

Other than the swift winds, still waters and daffodils across our lands;

Her hips are still considered His greatest creation."

Her hips being that of a woman, men glazed upon her. We extract features from her to describe her beauty. This woman, made from rib. Even though she competes over beauty with Mother Nature, the daffodils the swift winds, this beautiful land, her hips are life and life is God's greatest creation.

"Into the world is given a boy and a girl, and we should cry and accept what her hips give us."

God's greatest creation, life itself, the very thing we have as we wake. The breath we take the mourning and sorrow when it's taken away. Born into this world is continued life; little boys and little girls. We should cry, knowing this innocent child will one day have to face life, and then one day face death.

This is what her hips give us. She gives us life and everything that comes with it, good or bad.

> *"Yet we leap for joy only to ignore, refusing to take notice of her flaws.*
>
> *For she is complicated,"*

I stated before she is unpredictable. Knowing all of this we choose to ignore her flaws. We leap for joy and that is easy to understand why, but we must not forget how complex and complicated she is.

> *"Like the doves built around love, we somehow turn to the pigeons.*
>
> *Sad to say that we are ungrateful"*

Unpredictable, uncertainties, dangers, sorrow, secrets; these are words that can describe life's flaws. Aspiring, great, joyful, and adventurous; these are a few words to describe life's wonders. Starting to see how complicated she really is?

We leap for joy when welcoming a new life into the world yet we are ungrateful as well. In this example I mention doves. Doves are symbolic of love as they tend to fly together in couples. Try catching the sun's rays in camera view as a dove fly across. Is this beauty, this love which grounds our foundation not enough? Because somehow we turn to the pigeons, pigeons are categorized into the same family as doves. They come from the Columbidae species of birds. They are similar in appearance, just can be seen with different colors, typically green, gray and black or a mixture of all. That foundation that was built around love, like the doves, is then ruined by the betrayal of turning to another bird. We as humans can start something so sturdy, so powerful and have it broken down in an instance by something or someone else. This scenario is seen a lot in relationships and represents ungratefulness. In life, we tend to know what we want, yet still turn in other directions.

> *"Like the boy who can't appreciate the girl, but, Oh! How he loves her hips, only to dip in unable to make peace with"*

Continuing with this idea of being ungrateful, turning to the pigeons if you will. The boy loves the beauty the female has. He loves her curves and would love to have intercourse with her. Unable to truly see the value she possesses. In this aspect he is unable to make peace with her.

> *"Her hips are wide and also thick"*

Why live life being ungrateful? Life is wide and thick, simply put, life is full of itself. At this point in the poem we have seen her hips go from being tough to sharing abundance, to being God's greatest creation even against his creation of Mother Nature. She has given us new birth even throughout her flaws.

> *"But she is sometimes struck by ka-onde-onde,*
>
> *Getting thinner and thinner until she is no more*

*And during her ending stages, we would
finally see her hips as everything we lived for."*

Ka-onde-onde is an African slang term from
Zambia. The term means to get thin/something that
makes you thin. They are mostly referring to the HIV
virus that sickens its victims making them very ill and
thin like. I referenced *ka-onde-onde* to describe the
many things that could make your life thinner. Life is
full of itself but as we all know life can be struck by
illness, making your life shorter and shorter, until life
is no more. During that time we would finally see that
this life, her hips, is everything we lived for.

*"That twist, that shake, that lovely walk that
flashes between space and vision."*

Passing time life continued to twist, her hips
shaking and moving as vividly as we continue to
dance with her, our memories, our actions all flashing
before our eyes. Between space (everything in front
of us), and vision (our eyes) we are close to losing
her. They say before you die your life will flash, and
you will be able to see all of the things that you have
done and wanted to do. Live with her when she is
wide and thick.

So as we approach the end of the poem, as we
did throughout this review, we see that her hips are
life and we must seize every opportunity we have
with her and be prosperous.

"Because simply her hips are life and every night I slept with her, seizing her prosperous form. For that body of hers is all that I need."

Live life to the fullest and be grateful of the life you live. Make the most of your time here on earth. This is the message I received after I wrote this poem. Out of this collection I would have to say that this one is one of my favorites. I hope your interpretation of this poem meant something to you as well, and I hope that you received some form of inspiration after this review.

The Tree Series

Three Part Poem Series

Children of Sin

I dreamed a hill a field at far,

Abound its tops children frolicked and danced about.

Each to hush secrets keep,

Three children will sing to me.

One being stubborn with foolish pride,

Living a lie though he cries inside.

The next to sing depressed and alone,

Eating the scraps of a *doglets** bone.

Ignoring the fullness of fruit and the fish at sea,

Only to devour peasants meat through gluttony.

The last song was worst of all,

Melodies that made the children weep.

Afraid of whips and bonds did cause a fuss,

Melodies from the haunting pleasures of lust.

As each song made my soul seem weak,

The children suddenly hung from a tree.

So till this day as I awake from a sleepless rest,

Only to reflect these sins that destroys my flesh.

A Poet's Psalm

My path is lost and my soul is weary.

As I commit deeper into transgression.

Ashamed of such a life, so to a thousand cares I once sung.

To keep thy servant away from willful sin. (Psalms 19)

To carry this burden for I had no Simon of Cyrene,

Only to feel the kiss of Judas.

As I accompany myself to the branches of this guilty tree.

For I no longer want to weep this poet's psalm.

The Weeping Tree

In a field full of disbelief,

Where the wind flows of melancholy.

There, standing was a tangible soul,

Standing tall in a pensive thought.

Accompanied by branches, encased as one as one for each,

There lies a weeping tree.

To live or to die?

To live or to die?

Though it's rare the fog does clear,

To see the tree is I.

Weary and consumed by despair.

To live or to die?

To live or to die?

*** End of Series***

The Tree Series Review

"I dreamed a hill a field at far.

Abound its tops children frolicked and danced about.

Each to hush a secrets keep,

Three children will sing to me."

In this series it is important to note that the children represent the tone needed to drive each poem forward. They are the subject, the bases of the author that leads to his despair. These children which are his transgression leads to the dismal field where his soul is resting found in ***"The Weeping Tree."*** The author dreams of a hill where three children, three transgressions will reveal themselves. The children are frolicking around, dancing about, waiting to sing of these secrets that will soon haunt him later.

But before we can understand his particular sin, we must first define what it means to transgress. Sin is considered to go against divine law. In many religions those laws are defined as any act against the divine law, this is what sin is; but what if I'm not religious, then what? Sin can also be defined as seven traits or seven deadly sins. Though these seven deadly sins align themselves with religion, particularly in the origin of Christianity, it also could be considered universal, mythological, sort of like astrology. The seven deadly sins are Pride/Vanity, Envy, Gluttony, Lust, Anger, Greed and Sloth.

A great poet by the name of Dante Alighieri depicted what we have used as descriptions of hell in his epic poem **"The Divine Comedy."** Part one of that poem titled **"The Inferno,"** detailed his descent in to hell depicting it as having nine-circles. Those descriptions are part of what I used to describe hell in **"Inspirational Orbs"** each circle representing a particular sin.

So as we see the first child reveals himself as pride, the author is living a lie inside and his pride is leading him to cry. The next child sings a song of gluttony. What we put in our bodies, what we indulge in has a significant amount of what makes us who we are, the desire to consume more than what is required is gluttony. This child is singing a depressing song eating scraps and slop that isn't even fit for a dog, the author ignoring fruit and fish to eat peasant's meat. Before I converted into being an Israelite I use to eat swine and all food that was deemed unworthy in religious eyes: pork and bottom feeders to name a couple. The feeling I received after eating that type of food left me to feel disgusted inside.

The last song was the worst for the author that made the rest of his transgressions weep, this song of lust, plaguing his love, his mind, encompassing his guilt. This lust which leads to greed, envy and even anger; lusting for more (greed), envious of who he doesn't have, angry at not receiving his desires, spurning away love.

So as each child sings their song, suddenly the guilt of the author takes the lives of the children, they are now hanging from the tree. Symbolizing the sins that now encases him, they destroy his flesh.

Poet's Psalm.

"My path is lost and my soul is weary.

As I commit deeper into transgression"

So at the end of ***"Children of Sin"*** the author is now awake, fully aware of his transgressions. He now realizes that his path is lost. What he does next is the whole idea of good deeds, hoping that if he could help others then he could find his path again.

"Ashamed of such a life, so to a thousand cares I once sung.

To keep thy servant away from wilfull sin (Psalms 19)"

One thousand cares is what he tries to give. He hopes to keep his peers away from sin with the whole idea that "you are guilty by association." In psalms 19 it speaks of keeping your servants away from sin so that you may go blamelessly. In other words keep those around you safe and away from danger/ bad acts, in this case sin, so that you are not liable. The author tries to use this knowledge to help others, but what happens only causes more grief for him.

"To carry this burden for I had no Simon of Cyrene

Only to feel the kiss of Judas"

He now carries the burden of trying to save others. So to give an example I referenced Jesus Christ carrying the cross being symbolic of the burden to save God's people. In this poem referring to this reference, we see that Christ had Simon to help carry that cross, to help carry the burden. The author in this poem has no help, he is left to try and save his peers from transgression by himself and in doing so just like Christ, and he is betrayed. Judas being known for his treachery betrayed Jesus Christ with a kiss in exchange for 30 pieces of silver. So as the author is carrying this burden he is left to feel that same kiss from his peers. This leaves him hopeless, accompanying himself to branches to the guilty tree. He now becomes one with that branch, hanging; committing what appears to be suicide.

"As I accompany myself to the branches of this guilty tree.

For I no longer want to weep this poet's psalm."

The Weeping Tree

In the weeping tree we finally reach the end of the author's journey battling his transgression. He has now hung himself, but isn't dead just yet. There is still time for him to live. As he is one with the tree he asks should I live or should I die?

In a field full of sorrow we begin to see the author, full of despair, full of melancholy. He is standing there is a pensive thought, the key word being to stand, he hasn't committed suicide just yet. He simply is accompanied by the branch but is not lifted from whatever surface that is grounding him.

"There, standing was a tangible soul,

Standing tall in a pensive thought.

Accompanied by branches, encased as one as one for each,

There lies a weeping tree.

To live or to die?"

In a deep, contemplative thought he is battling between removing that surface or removing the rope that has him with the branches of the tree, to live or to die, to live or to die?

Does he end like the children in his dream? Were they revealing to him his transgression or were they trying to reveal to him his destiny and fate? I end the poem with that question.

Does the author lives or decides to die? I, myself being the author of this poem, it is clear that I am living, but this poem is for those who is battling suicide, that has pressure suffocating their mind leading to depression and despair. I ask of you to please live.

Dedicated to all that have taken their lives and those who currently live with suicidal thoughts; we hear your screams, we see your pain, you are not alone. There are reasons to live,

Much Love, Hope and Happiness.

End of Review

Desolate Dreams

My love appeared to me in a dream.

In a place so far from where I lay my head.

A place where love remains dreams,

A place far from my bed.

I once dreamt of her; a lucid dream,

My body paralyzed though I felt her spirit near.

She moaned with me she wiped my tears,

My love so far from here.

Her womb of fertile yoke and her breast I needed to tend.

Her lips that locked in place with mines,

Lust or love I can't admit.

In a desolate place where dreams begin,

Is the same place where this dream end.

Robert's Julia

Upon her clothes tell Herrick I see,

This promiscuous garment that stands before me.

How sweet you say her glittering vibrations go?

For I sense the spice in how she flows.

Her clothes, oh her clothes!

She settles in her stance,

To lift her drapes while time is at hand.

Now upon her skin I am eager to take this chance.

To take her body and enjoy this dance.

Robert's Julia Review

Robert Herrick (1591-1674) was a caviler poet of his time known for his vivid poems about love, nature, divine spirituality and carpe diem. ***"To the Virgins to Make Much of Time"*** has been featured in literature books for students in high school and was prominently featured in **Dead Poets Society** starring Robin Williams. That poem in particular focused on seizing the opportunity while time is at hand, and while that may be one of his most popular poems themed around carpe diem; his poems about and to his love Julia is what inspired ***"Robert's Julia."***

"Upon her clothes tell Herrick I see"

This line opens up with my response/rendition to Robert Herrick's ***"Upon Julia Clothes."*** In this particular poem to Julia he describes her garments as flowing so smooth and gracefully. She is near perfect in Robert's eyes. Her clothes are liquefied and the site of her sends vibrations as he writes *"That liquefaction of her clothes; that brave vibration each way free."*[9]

So Julia, being his love during his time flowed sweetly, her garments being awe-inspiring. So tell Herrick that I do see her as well, but now in my time, in my views her clothing is now promiscuous. I used his poem and my poem to describe how women have changed over the span of about 350 years.

Women dressing more traditionally during Herrick's years; now dressing with more appeal. Just as in his poem Julia was described as being vibrant, flowing smooth and sweet. Ah! Yes that is perfectly fine just as how my Julia is described as being spicy in her vibrancy and flow.

> *"How sweet you say her glittering vibrations go?*
>
> *For I sense the spice in how she flows"*

My Julia has grown to be very different than how Robert viewed her. She is feisty and sassy in the way she walks. Her clothes reveal to me of all her sexy ways.

No mention in ***"Upon Julia Clothes"*** where Herrick seizes the chance to take Julia. Ironic because he is known for carpe diem, but he does mention that her glittering takes him. Is this just the site of Julia taking him? In my rendition Julia has settled in her stance. She is being feisty (spicy) sassy and promiscuous and that catches my eye, it takes me. So here is my opportunity to take my chance with her

> *"To lift her drapes while time is at hand*
>
> *Now upon her skin I am eager to take this chance*
>
> *To take her body and enjoy this dance"*

Instead of being upon her clothes I have made my move to be upon her skin, Julia is now naked waiting for me to enjoy what she has to offer. She once took Robert as he wrote *"glittering that taketh me"* but I choose to take her. I am eager, anxious, and ready to share this moment of affection, passion and excitement.

She has been spicy since I've seen her, she has been promiscuous and with these heated moments, we must share this dance, we must have intercourse. So yes tell Herrick that I see Julia as she lies before me.

Prayer, Oh lord Just

No rain for me,

From the highest mountains to the lowest hills,

In which I lived.

Oh lord please forgive me.

Or send me to Calvary if need be,

Though I ask that you send me there with serenity.

So as I pass the crossroads,

Bless me the eyes to see,

So when the serpent speaks I will realize his lies as he tries to strike down my deity.

Send me the waters that washes sin,

So that I am walking with the purist soul tainted by the blood of your son.

Am I relieved?

To the highest mountains in which I have reached,

No storms I fear.

So from here I send this prayer,

Oh lord just hear.

Secrets

With the passing of coming days,

I wish I could reverse the hour glass going one score

back.

Beginning with my breath from the womb,

this curse I call it, and the whispers roam.

Why do we lie? Because the truth is sometimes what

we fear,

so by lying we hide the fact that we are afraid.

Our secrets are only our seeking moments of our

hidden selves.

It's only normal that we judge,

placing false perceptions amongst one another.

So my skin and my mask,

enables me to hide from my brother.

My voice is loud and as quiet as a whisper.

Genuine can never seek.

I'm a walking closet,

and skeleton underneath.

My cover couldn't block the rain,
when the acid would fall,
soon burning my skin, it revealed my skeleton and all.
Hiding, but with so many pairs of eyes, judgment still
finds us.

So with the passing of coming time,
if I could rewind my clock, going back to the start.
I would take away the skin, mask, whispers, and this
false image,
finally allowing my brothers to judge my heart.
Let's shatter our mask, and erase our secrets.

Dawn's Air

Gather ye thoughts, as we lay,

To comfort me like Dawn's Air.

So when the rose pedals tend to float and flow like
the rivers,

Time will tell.

That my love is love's reflection;

*Ere** the nights

We'll count the days to seize this affection we share.

So gather my heart I give for you to heal,

To keep it warm and true.

To comfort me like Dawn's Air.

Dawn's Air Review

Gather up your thoughts as we are lying together and comfort me. The message laid out throughout this poem was to signify the comfort of coming into a new day out of darkness, to signify a breath of fresh air by living in a new relationship.

Rose pedals are very symbolic in relation to love. The imagery I used to have my rose pedals floating upstream, being river-like is to show the growth of this new love. Then time again will reveal that this love of mine is love's reflection. She is the embodiment of what love should be and what love should look like.

"Ere the nights,

We'll count the days to seize this affection we share"

Dawn being the start of a new day, it is important to seize those days. My love and I are counting the days together, counting as we share this thought. Before the night, we count, we grow, and we love, holding on to the affection that captures the essence of beginning something new.

While looking into relationships it is important to understand that no matter what happened before, a new day is sure to come. The comfort of dawn, coming out of that night, out of that darkness is sure to bring console. My character in this poem has found that comfort, placing him in bed lying with his lover in unity; together as one thought, as one adores the other. This poem was meant to remind those who are hurt, in and out of relationships that there's still a new day. There's still someone out there that could offer comfort and affection.

"So gather my heart I give for you to heal

To keep it warm and true

To comfort me like Dawn's Air."

Harmony of the Wind

I smile whenever she smiles

As she glides so smoothly into spring

For she is nature's compliment

As swift like the air and mist I breathe

I needed for her to fall into my arms like an autumn's breeze

As her warmth has a grasp on me

Pulling me inside her thighs

To make me feel as though I am one with the summer time

Skipping over winters for her love is never so cold

Oh baby!

Could she be the harmony of the wind?

Violet's Garden

My prayers to *Eros* reeked of a scent from a beautiful garden.

Though no nose could physically smell,

Alas! He blessed me the sight of a purple morning.

This beautiful flower which blossomed overnight,

I awoke to witness astonishing love.

Her pedals flying amongst the wind,

I seen her smile, and I felt her power.

Together we silenced applauds,

That was thrown into disbelief.

Hatred if you will towards her and me.

I, hiding my feelings away,

I couldn't allow her to be ruined,

For this moment I stood in her garden,

Waiting for us to blossom as one.

Then *Eros*, as swift as he brought her near

Took my love's garden and gave her to another man.

Violet's Garden Review

"My prayers to Eros reeked of a scent from a beautiful garden"

In Greek mythology Eros is the god of love. To understand his importance in this poem is to first glance at many myths surrounding his name. One myth being that he is blindfolded while carrying a bow and arrow able to make anyone he strikes fall in love with the first person they see. This is where I want to expand; if Eros can force this love on someone to whomever they see first, this indicates a lack of control towards that person who is falling in love.

Let me explain further, I used Eros to signify how we as humans cannot 'help' who we fall in love with or have feelings for. We all have our standards or a particular type that we go for, but when it comes to love it can be very tricky. The Romans believed Eros to be Cupid, that's the name we tend to give him in today's time.

Cupid struck me with his bow, allowing me to reek of this new profound love of mine. At the sight of this flower blossoming overnight, I immediately fell in love (love at first site).

"I awoke to witness astonishing love.

Her pedals flying amongst the wind,

I seen her smile, and I felt her power."

How powerful is the love? I mean I can feel the power she expresses behind her smile. I cannot turn away; her embodiment has me trapped under a spell it seems. Her love is as swift as the pedals that paint over the everglades and field plains, awakening to witness this love.

"Together we silenced applauds

That was thrown into disbelief

Hatred if you will towards her and me."

After all this affection and passion between her and me, I reveal that others do not agree with our relationship. Disbelief I describe it, though it has no effect on us, together we simply silence what others think, and yes this love of mine will forever have my heart, but I could not let this hatred from others ruin her. To see us together will be discussed as a mockery to what is right.

"I couldn't allow her to be ruined

For this moment I stood in her garden,

Waiting for us to blossom as one."

I had no choice but to put my feelings to the side so that she would be saved, hoping that one day we would blossom without the negativity behind our connection. And as soon as Eros brought my love to me he also took her away, leaving me to wish and wait, while she belongs to another man.

The Tree That Grew For Me

I suffered thy tree,

That was afraid to grow.

As it cried out for me,

The heavy burden of sheltering the birds to sing.

 I suffered thy tree,

That screamed to me,

"Please protect me from torture of axes and chains,

I do not want to bleed."

I suffered thy tree,

That reached out to me

Its tiny branches hugging the sun's warmth,

Praying to be free.

I suffered thy tree,

That sung to me,

The day my Grandfather planted its seed.

Though when he passed,

I suffered and continued to weep,

Remembering all the things he taught to me.

The responsibility to provide shelter.

The strength to heal wounds.

The perseverance to reach goals.

And when I lifted my head,

This tree was no longer afraid.

For as strong as I grew

I no longer suffered thy tree,

Because all along it was growing for me.

The Tree That Grew For Me Review

Dedicated to Horace Seaborne

This poem is dear to my heart; it is dedicated to my grandfather. The gift to write, tell stories and write poems came from the teaching from pops. I can remember the days where he would tell me stories of his youth, his fatherhood and I would watch him do yard work, and build to expand his home. In my eyes it was nothing he couldn't do. I remember one particular story he told me where his son had planted a tree in the yard. He watched that tree grow to be as old as him before he passed, but the tree wasn't the only thing growing.

All along I was growing with that same tree. In life there is a moment we must face responsibility. Responsibility may cause us to be afraid, cause us to suffer. The tree that grew for me represents the challenges in life we may face. Sheltering the birds to sing, shelter is a necessity that adds a burden to some lives. Protection from the axes and chains that destroys trees is symbolic of the pain that could possibly destroy lives. All these things that the tree suffered are something that we all could suffer from. But I had Horace Seaborne to teach me responsibility, perseverance, and the ability to heal wounds. Because of him I am not afraid.

The Argument of God

I look up; show me spirit,

They look over to show me man.

I close my eyes; pray to him to witness miracles,

They dig deeper to show me working hands.

I show them water,

They point out charts,

"Explanation is best to give"

I hear them speak,

I sense their knowledge.

Yet I still fear,

For if I'm wrong and only then,

Will I interred away to make amends.

But if you're wrong and he does exist,

Then there's a challenge on your hands.

The Argument of God Review

The Argument of God is simply constructed as a back and forth debate. Everything I mention in terms of belief is then argued by either man or science. This poem is not meant to recruit believers or condemn non-believers, but to simply bring awareness to this debate that dates thousands of years back.

Since the introduction of a supreme being there has always been a counter into existence. God created the Heavens and the Earth, the animals and man, the universe was created by **The Big Bang Theory.** You see for every explanation into having a God there is a counter explanation. This debate sparked my interest once I read a poem by Robert Herrick, a poet mentioned in **"Robert's Julia Review."** The poem is titled *"To Find God"* where he task his readers to complete impossible challenges.

He opens his poem by challenging us (the reader) to weigh fire and measure wind,

> *"Weigh me the fire; or canst thou find a way to measure out the wind."*

-Herrick[9]

I understand that fire cannot be weighed and wind cannot be measured but it's those challenges that bring up the question as to where the author is trying to take me? If man cannot do these particular challenges then who can?

"To Find God" is a poem that holds true to not trying to convince the reader of finding God, but more so as to reveal the mysteries and wonders that has been created. The author's tone in this poem is not to persuade the reader that there is a God, but to simply bring awareness about the existence of God. For instance the last two lines of the poem:

> *"This if thou canst, then show me him. That rides the glorious Cherubim."*[*]

-Herrick[9]

Many challenges he elaborates on such as; count the sands and dust,

> *"or fetch me back that cloud again, Beshiver'd into seeds of rain."*

-Herrick[9]

These things we all know cannot be completed. So in the last lines the author's points are that, if you can't (canst) do these challenges then show me him (God) someone who can. I know I can't weigh fire as I stated but I know it's real, same as I can't see God but he must be real. The author allowed the reader to come to this conclusion without force feeding that God exists.

So in my rendition of this poem, or what was influenced by *"To Find God"* came about *"The Argument of God."* I start my argument by stating that as I look up I see spirit, but then they will show me man. This opening statement sets up the debate to follow. For everything I believe to be spirit will be countered by everything that is man.

> *"I pray to witness miracles,*
>
> *They dig deeper to show me working hands"*

For what I believe to be miracles can simply be countered by the success of men. For instance if I believe someone having a surgical operation done and they heal from it and there were no complications, most believers will say that that was the work of God. Others may simply thank the doctor who was the overseer of the operation. This debate continues throughout the poem. I show them water, they show me charts. Scientific explanations to how water is formed, even to the point of creating it themselves. Water is H^2O, hydrogen to oxygen.

> *"I sense their knowledge"*

This idea of God versus Man continues to the point where even I decided to give in. So I ended the poem in a fashion similar to Herrick. Instead of asking for those who failed at his challenges to show him God, I simply state that if I'm wrong and God does not exist. Then I will go away quietly to inter or be buried once I'm dead to simply make amends, to simply rest in my change peacefully. But if you're wrong and God does exist, then the challenge of the afterlife will have to be on your hands.

A Slave's Response to His Master

Take away the chains that keep me from reaching you,

And I ask what power do you have?

Keep your holsters filled with grief,

Instead of weapons,

And I'm sure you'll beg to me,

For the power you wish you had.

I'll even surround you three hundred and fifty nine degrees.

To leave a little hope,

Hope to escape my power in which I have always held,

Power in which you seek.

See it's easy to see,

That without your guns and your fancy speech,

There's nothing you could've ever done... to me.

A Slave's Response to His Master Review

This continuous battle for power over the next man is where I got the idea to place myself in the shoes of my ancestors. Power: defined as the ability to do something or act in a particular way, especially as a faculty or quality. So what is power over someone? Is it respected which in turn could be fear? Fear itself; being a displacement originating from something or somewhere. For instance the fear of death, if I could control the moment someone will die, I could possibly tap into that fear of death thus having power over them. So in the history of slave owners and slaves; the control over a life created power, this poem being the response to that power.

"Take away the chains and bonds that keep me from reaching you"

Without these limitations to freely be, represented by the chains and bonds that restrain ligaments control is then implemented. Take those away then what? The next line of this poem is then presented as aggression. It is safe to assume that this slave is not controlled by fear.

"And I ask what power do you have?"

This rebellious mindset led to many battles between slave and slave owners, one in particular in American history, the rebellion of Nat Turner. Now without restraints, the slave has to hurdle the power of weapons. In this poem I speak of fire power.

"Keep your holsters filled with grief, instead of weapons and I'm sure you'll beg to me for the power in which you had."

Though this slave is not controlled by fear he understands that weapons could over power him. So he tells his master to fill their holsters with grief, with distress, contrite over the annihilation of a man instead of the weapons that caused this grief and destruction in the first place. Without the control of fear, the restraints of chains and without weapons, this master would beg for the power he thought he had.

"I'll even surround you three-hundred and fifty nine degrees, to leave a little hope"

Surrounding your enemy is like backing a deer into a corner. Eventually they'll be forced to fight back. Why take this chance? Surround you enemy, but also leave an opening for them to flee. The concern over the slave's master resonates with compassion. This is how to defeat power generated by control and fear. "You kept me in bonds and chains, you used your weapons against me, but why should I be the same as you?" My power doesn't come from those fearing me but those who respect me. Power in this form is what the master sought.

"So it's easy to see that without your guns and your fancy speech, there's nothing you could have ever done to me."

Fancy speech; language barriers is a way to also exhort control. My intelligence is deemed as unusual when I'm faced with the majority of those who speak differently than me. This does not make me un-intelligent just blocks me behind a barrier. Some become obsessed with the phenomenon of language thus crafting change into their lives to either impress those in whom they want to be or to exalt a brief understanding into the lives of others through understanding that language. How did this phenomenon play a role with slavery? Take someone away from their native tongue and they will be forced against said barrier. Slaves were not un-intelligent, just weren't proficient in the "fancy speech" that we call English. Being an African American man, my whole life I spoke English, I write in its literacy. Ask me to read memoirs in French or Arabic and I wouldn't have the slightest clue of where to begin. Am I un-intelligent? The answer is no, but I have the capability to learn either French or Arabic. Slaves were not allowed to read the language used in America. This inflicts once again, control and power.

The slave in this poem understands that if you take away that speech, weapons and chains, then no power would've ever been granted.

Possession of a Poet

Spirits wander in wantonness

Searching for men to possess

For when they reach a poet's doorstep

That's when his words are expressed

Possession of a Poet Review

Every since I started writing poetry I always believed that my words came from another realm, my ideals, my visions, my poetry spurring from deep within; I myself not knowing where to begin, challenging myself to even write reviews for majority of the poems. When I decided to write *"The Devil's Narrative,"* each poem came to me years apart and not in sequence. The same with *"The Tree Series;"* I didn't plan for those poems to go together in any type of series. Once I saw that they were themed around a certain message, a certain subject then that's when I decided to fit them together. Each poem written at separate times in my life, joined together as one. Was it because I heard the narrative of Lucifer at each stage in my life or envisioned sin whaling amongst trees? Spirits I believe coming to me in a dream just the same as angels/God came to *Isaiah, Jacob, Job, Samuel, Sarah and Moses.*[*]

"Spirits wander in wantonness"

I believe that spirits seek out writers, and in my case poets. Ever had a chill come down your spine while writing something so profound, so reflective? Ever read something that gave you those feelings; spirits maybe? They search in wantonness, inflicting what I believe to be deeper than just pain. This poem was not set out to describe the thoughts of a poet but the origin of his words. So what pain does he feel? Talk to any writer and I test you to ask him of his beset mind. This pain, this agony of words placed on paper to soon become a man's legacy. The disquiet of that alone, the intricacy of that pedestal creates insanity within a sane man. These spirits that haunts him which haunts me, is that Shinigami?

"Searching for men to possess"

This four line poem, details more than the quantity of its length. Why these spirits searching and what are they searching for? They are seeking possession. The origin of my words does not come from me alone. Credited to whoever fell short of deities, roaming the world waiting to be graced by paradise, these ghostly spirits that live in my mind; yelling while pulling themselves out of my sub-conscience in hopes that their expressions could come to life. These men, women and children with a story to tell, seek out a vessel. These spirits helped piece together two series in this collection; they helped with the poetic devices found within this collection. The imagery, the depth, all came from being possessed.

"When they reach a poet's doorstep

That's when his words are expressed"

Tempus Fugit

Does a bird sing to fly?

Or just spread its wings?

Does a moth wander to the light,

Wishing to die?

Is time the record holder?

In the glorious lamps that race.

Some days the sun would win,

Some nights the moon.

But never do they tie.

What if I told you to wait and sing?

Before your future could be bright.

I assume you'll reply I cannot sing, so waiting would
be a lie.

Time is the record holder.

But chance he tends to give.

So race against the sun and moon.

Succeed or fail then succeed again.

Tempus Fugit Review

Does a bird sing to fly? As we all know a bird doesn't sing to fly, they just, fly. The idea of carpe diem, seizing the day highly influenced this poem. Each question throughout this poem brings up the idea to just do it. A bird doesn't need to sing to fly, we as humans don't need to just speak about it but actually take advantage of doing whatever it is we set out to accomplish. In order to write a book, you must first write or in order to produce a song you must have a song to produce. The flight of the bird is used to represent the height of our accomplishments, the place we all would like to be in our lives. Well how does the bird get there? Simple, they simply spread their wings and go. Well how can we get there? Again, simple, just go.

Well aren't there risks involved? Yes, there are risks in everything we do in life, but the flight of the bird is the goal correct? Well the attraction of the light is the goal set for the moth. *"Does a moth wonder to the light, wishing to die?"* The attraction alone is what the moth sees, the grasp that the light has is too hard for the moth to turn away from. It loves what it sees; it wants what it sees, so it travels towards the light. Not every light bulb kills insects, see there's risk to going after what you want. Some risk may hurt you while others won't. The moth doesn't know that may be a zapper he is headed towards, but the mere magnetism of the light itself symbolizes his desires and wants. He has one life to live anyways why not give it a try? Sounds familiar?

"Is time the record holder?"

So is time the record holder? To answer that lets do one of my favorite exercises and "dig." The title ***"Tempus Fugit"*** is Latin for time flies.

"But Meanwhile time flies, flies irretrievably, while, captivated by passion, I describe each detail." Virgil Georgics: Book III: line 284[10]

In ***Georgics: Book III*** the poet Virgil speaks of agriculture, he speaks to the farmer. In that particular line he states that time flies irretrievably. We cannot capture time, yet he is captivated by passion, realizing the extent of time; time covering or being the overseer of the land (agriculture). The seasons are equivalent to time, the seasons dictating the land. Virgil writes of task that must be complete for when the colder seasons arise. For instance he speaks of lining the hard ground with straw and fern, so that the sheep aren't harmed by the chill of the ground; their feet won't suffer *"ugly foot-rot."* These themes remembering that time cannot be captured, cannot be retrieved still shows the labor of a farmer to ensure his profit, this, his passions. He writes, he speaks (the singing of birds) but also he simply does/task the farmer to do what needs to be done to protect the farmland. Time cannot be retrieved, so yes it is the record holder. It is the measurement of speed, the rotation of the earth, the measurement of the seasons. In this example these measurements control our agriculture, which in turn control our task needed to keep our land. Starting to see the importance of time? Don't put your shovels away just yet, keep digging.

"The glorious lamps that race"

The sun and the moon; we measure our days and nights by the rise and fall of the sun and moon. Some live in our days, others live in our nights. We cannot live through both. I cannot be in one part of the earth where there is day, and also be where there is night. A debate over this may be where the two connect over the seas, but even so, your life remains in either day or night. I cannot tip the hour glass, reversing time to do my days over or my nights.

"Some days the sun would win, some nights the moon."

So in continuation to taking risk, trying to fly, I encourage that we race against the sun and moon.

In *"To the Virgins to Make Much of Time"* by Robert Herrick he personified the sun by making it race. From the time it arises in the east and sets in the west we must make the most of our time.

"But never do they tie."

Your days and nights will never be the same, never fall at the same time. Make the most of what you have. When I ask you to wait and sing before your future could be bright; for those who cannot sing would think of this as nonsense. If I asked a bird to sing before they could fly, they would just take off on me. Flapping away leaving me to stand there looking foolish. "Why should we wait in the first place?" They would ask. I find it easier to simply seize the opportunity. Time is the record holder; opportunity will come, be like the birds and just fly and be like the moth going for what you want. You will succeed, you will fail, but I assure you that you will succeed again. Try and continue to try because time does fly by.

"Time is the record holder.

But chance he tends to give.

So race against the sun and moon.

Succeed or fail then succeed again" *Tempus Fugit*

33: March 27th 1992

By the age of thirty-three I will leave my message where the messenger left off,

Though I pray he forgives me for my blasphemy.

33: March 27th 1992 Review

Small trivia or fun fact before we get started with this particular poem; *"33, March 27th 1992"* was the original title for this collection of poems; every since I started writing poetry, I always prophesized that by the age of 33 my message through poetry would be my stamp into the world. Looking at the number 33 in a religious standpoint, we see that many believe that Jesus Christ died at that age. Well his gospel in the text is the ultimate message.

"Though I pray he forgives me for my blasphemy"

This small two line poem creates more than the length of the poem itself. I pray for forgiveness for even challenging his message. To think that I could be as powerful as he ever was through words; my poetry reflects many aspects of life as if we were reading the bible. 33 encompass my entire message, bringing my prophecy to life. Later I changed the title to *"**The Argument of Butterflies**"* due to the symbolism and significance of butterflies. Butterflies represent the life cycle, adapting to change, even reflection after growth. All of these things can be found through my poetry.

I enjoyed each phase of this process, from creating the message to bringing my words to life with reviews. This is my power, my words, my message and my prophecy. I hope you guys enjoyed

Brandon Taliaferro

The Argument of Butterflies

I wonder of crystals through cyclic form?

Or diamonds aging in mystery.

If the catacombs were never filled,

And there was no expiration given, no need for reincarnation.

Then would diamonds be so marvelous?

I wonder of grace, untainted by mercy.

Never sharing a moment of existence.

The mystery of whom and what we are,

Being merely myths, legends of our own creation.

I wonder of birth,

Particularly wombs and lungs.

Revealing breath and growth

Knowledge of fruit and debate of song.

I wonder and yes I wonder,

Ah! The Argument of Butterflies.

<u>The Argument of Butterflies</u>

Where the Messenger Left Off

Notes*

Cherubim: The glorious Cherubim as found in "To Find God" by Robert Herrick is a celestial being. A winged angel describe in biblical text to attend to God.

Doglets Bone: An old southern term that means to feed someone dog scraps/dog slop

Ere: Means before in broken or old English

Sheol's door: Hell/Hades/The Gates of Hell

Temeluchus: Found in the Apocalypse of Paul the apostle; Temeluchus was the overseer/care taker of children as well as the chief tormentor of the damned.

Turtle's back: The mystical ideals of the earth's creation being the growth of the turtle's back.

Shinigami: Ghost/spirit/Death God mostly used in Japanese culture

Jacob, Moses, Samuel, Isaiah: Biblical men found in the bible to have had dreams with either God or his Angels.

Appendix

[4]Brown, Dan. "Angels and Demons" novel 2009.

[1]Darwin, Charles. *The origins of species*. New York: P. F. Collier & son, 1937. Print.

[9]Herrick, Robert, and M. K. Pace. *Delight in Disorder: Selected Poems*. Maidstone: Crescent Moon, 2007. Print.

[5,6,7,8]King James: Holy Bible. Matthew 8:31, Matthew 7:13, Luke 16:19-31, Luke 16:26

[3]Phillips, Jonathan. "The Crusades: A Complete History | History Today." N.p., n.d. Web. 23 Oct. 2016.

[2]Sharī'atī, 'Alī, Laleh Bakhtiar, and Andrew Burgess. *Religion vs religion*. Place of publication not identified: ABC International Group, 2000. Print.

[10]Virgil, and A. S. Kline. "Virgil." *Virgil (70 BC–19 BC) - The Georgics: Book III*. Livestock Farming, 2001. Web. 24 Dec. 2016.